KENDRA SIMS

I'M SAVED BUT I STRUGGLE

A Realistic Look at Salvation

Teri,
Thank you for investing in me!
God loves you and is proud to claim
you as His daughter! Continue to
do His work and your reward will
be great because it will come from
God. ♡ Kendra L. Sims, author

Limits of Liability and Disclaimer of Warranty

The author and publisher shall not be liable for your misuse of this material. This book is strictly for informational and educational purposes. The purpose of this book is to educate and entertain. The author and/or publisher do not guarantee that anyone following these techniques, suggestions, tips, ideas, or strategies will become successful. The author and/or publisher shall have neither liability nor responsibility to anyone with respect to any loss or damage caused, or alleged to be caused, directly or indirectly by the information contained in this book.

Views expressed in this publication do not necessarily reflect the views of the publisher.

Printed in the United States of America.

ISBN 978-1-948270-13-7
Keen Vision Publishing, LLC
www.keen-vision.com

Your struggle season matters.

-Kendra Sims

CONTENTS

INTRODUCTION

Hello Readers,

Disclaimer: *This is NOT a self-help book. This is a God-help-me book.*

From the first glance of this book, I bet you hesitated to pick it up, put it in your Amazon cart, or click download on Kindle. Upon reading the title, you probably thought to yourself, *"Oh gosh, not another Holy-Ghost-filled-fire-baptized writer who thinks she can tell me how I need to get it together and live right."* Yet, you find yourself reading the pages to see what this book is all about. I'm certainly glad you did.

I'm far from perfect. I know all too well of the battle to live the life Christ died for us to live. I don't always feel like being a prayer warrior, going to church, being nice to others, and all the other things we are expected to do as believers. I love God, and I want Him to be proud of me, but in the same breath, there are areas in which I struggle as well. I imagine that this is where you currently find yourself – loving God, but still struggling. While I don't profess to know all the answers, I'm certain that my journey thus far has provided me with clarity and insight about a few of the areas in which most believers face difficulty. So, my friend, I'm here to lend a helping hand and provide you with as much as I know to help you on this journey. For starters, there is a thin line between *living* for God and *flirting* with Satan. If we are honest, sometimes we do things to create the illusion that we are living for God. We go to church, pay our tithes, and even volunteer with the children's ministry. However, deep down inside, we're not as *all in* as we know we should be.

"So, because you are lukewarm, and neither hot nor cold, I will spit you out of my mouth."
Revelation 3:16 (ESV)

I don't know about you, but that scripture always makes me reconsider my actions, thoughts, and speech. Upon reading it, I always ask myself, "Kendra, are you lukewarm?" Have you ever tasted lukewarm coffee, hot chocolate, or tea? The taste is extremely dissatisfying. Just as you wouldn't like to consume lukewarm beverages that are supposed to be hot, God does not want children who half-serve, half-submit, or half-obey Him. He wants all of us, and rightfully so.

After all, He did create us and sacrifice His Son so that we may live. Ponder this question for a moment: *Where's the fulfillment in being a lukewarm Christian?* This question is difficult for many of us to answer. Even though we feel the tugging deep within us to be more, do more, and sacrifice more, it's easy to remain in our comfortable routines of half-living for Christ. My friend, though it may be pleasing to our flesh, this kind of unfulfilling lifestyle will ultimately lead to our dissatisfaction with everything we do or commit ourselves to. It doesn't matter how many magazine clippings we attach to our vision boards, if our hearts are not transformed, we will remain unfulfilled.

In this book, I will discuss many of the actions and behaviors of believers that point back to the world instead of our Creator. This book will challenge you to take inventory of what's in your heart and mind. As we journey through, feel free to write notes or highlight things you need to work on or pray about! My prayer is that once you are done reading this book, you will be encouraged to live lives that are piping hot for Christ! If you're ready, turn the page and meet me in Chapter One!

Chapter One
WHAT BROUGHT YOU HERE?

As we discussed in the Introduction, the title of this book pretty much lets you know what this book is all about. Though it may have been difficult, you still saw the need to invest in this book. Maybe you didn't invest in it, and instead, someone purchased it for you. Maybe you found it online when you were shopping. Or, maybe you found it lying around somewhere and decided to give it a try. No matter how you happened upon this book, know that God is extremely intentional. He saw a need for it in your life. If you've made it past the Introduction, it's fair to say that you are really looking for some answers. Before we dig in, I want you to take a moment and think about why you felt the need to read this book. You're here for a reason, my friend! Why?

Have you figured it out? Great! Now, on a scale of 1 to 10, where would you rate your level of Christianity? Are you not quite a *one* but you wouldn't exactly give yourself an *eight*? I'm pretty sure the number you gave yourself was based on a personal assessment of the decisions you have made. Or, you did a swift reflection of your life and compared yourself to someone you consider a *ten*. Truth be told, we all have moments where our rating of our walk with Christ fluctuates. We go through seasons of being on fire for Christ and eager to learn more about Him and His Word. Then, there are seasons in which we just don't want to be bothered with the routine of being a Christian. Even if they never tell you, the person you may have compared yourself to goes through these seasons as well. As for you, what keeps you from being a *ten*? What causes you to go through seasons in which your submission to God wavers? Instead of *wishing* to attain a higher level of spirituality, how about *making the necessary changes* in your life so you can!

EXAMINATION

When was the last time you looked at yourself? No, not in the mirror. The view I'm referring to cannot be seen in a mirror. When was the last time you looked at your heart, motives, words, actions, and deeds? It's extremely easy to cover up our insecurities, hurt, heartbreak, impure motives, and sinful thoughts and actions. However, one of the first steps to becoming better is to examine ourselves and open ourselves to be examined by God. This is the only way we will ever be able to see the idols we have placed before God in our lives.

"Search me, O God, and know my heart; test me and know my anxious thoughts. Point out anything in me that offends you, and lead me along the path of everlasting life."

Psalm 139: 23-24 (NLT)

In Psalm 139, David praised God by acknowledging who He was and being thankful for His presence, love, grace, and other attributes. However, before ending this Psalm, David asked God to examine and analyze him for any habits that did not align with His Will. David's words in Psalm 139 confirms two things:

1. After the praise break, we must open our hearts to the work necessary for change.
2. In order for God to examine and convict us, we must be open to it. This can only be done through an intimate relationship with the Father.

If you've gone to church at least three times in your life, it's likely you've heard someone talk about David. King David is most known for his radical praise (1 Chronicles 15: 3-29), and his heart, love, and commitment to God. We often point out two facts about King David: how he worshipped, and how he went back to God after he made mistakes. However, what we sometimes fail to look at is how David opened himself up to be examined by God.

Scripture tells us that God knows us intimately and knitted us in our mother's womb.(Psalm 139:13) We know that we are not hidden from His view. God is all-knowing, and He is far from clueless about anything concerning His creations. So, why did David ask God to examine him? David wasn't asking God to just look at him. David was asking God to *look* and *tell* what He saw. **An observation is quite different from an examination.** When we observe a situation and even when we are observed, what is seen is not always communicated. However, if we go to our doctor and ask for an examination, we expect the doctor to communicate his findings. David opened himself for God to communicate about what He found in his heart. This is not an easy thing to do. However, it must be done if we desire to live on fire for God. Ask God to examine you. Ask Him to reveal the ugly parts, and trust Him to walk you through the steps of becoming clean.

Personally, I know I have made decisions that hurt God's feelings. In fact, when God showed me the error in my ways, it hurt even more. When God shows us where we need to make adjustments in our lives, we cannot sit and sulk in shame. We must do something about it! Typically, after God exposes the unclean areas of our hearts, the enemy attacks us with so much discouragement, that we sit and wallow in our mistakes instead of seeking God for deliverance. My friend, do not get stuck here! **The fact that disappointing God even breaks your heart is a sign that you care about what He thinks of you!** You wouldn't care if you sincerely did not desire to change. God is a deliverer. He can change and purify your heart. However, you must put in the work to stay delivered from the things that don't please our Father. If God shows you people you've put before Him, don't ask Him to remove them from your life if you're only going reach out and invite them back in. Don't ask God to take away your taste for liquor or drugs if you aren't willing to make adjustments to your routine. Don't ask to be delivered from porn if you refuse to cancel your subscriptions. You can't be delivered from anything you continue to make yourself available to. The longevity of any sin or burden in your life does not negate God's ability to intervene. There must be a willingness to change attached to intentional actions. in Ask God to search you so that He may expose and get rid of everything that separates you from Him!

SALVATION

> "If you declare with your mouth, "Jesus is Lord," and believe in your heart that God raised him from the dead, you will be saved. For it is with your heart that you believe and are justified, and it is with your mouth that you profess your faith and are saved."
>
> Romans 10:9-10 (NIV)

My home church often had week-long youth conferences during the summer. One year, I attended, and my mind was transformed about the meaning of salvation. All that week, I felt a pull on my heart to become an official member of God's family. When I told my mom about it, she smiled and said, "Well, Pooh, why don't you wait until Sunday and walk down to the altar when pastor opens the doors of the church?" *(Note: Opening the doors of the church means inviting people to receive salvation or join the church.)* When my mother asked that question, I smiled at her nervously. Truth be told, the thought of walking down to the altar made me nauseous. I imagined people looking at me and formulating their own opinions. The thought of a full congregation staring at me was enough to make me anxious and uncomfortable. On the last day of the youth conference, in the summer of 2001, I waited until most of the sanctuary was clear and my mother nudged me to speak to the pastor. In a soft, timid voice, I told the pastor that I was interested in joining the church. He smiled and asked, "Are you saved?"

"I don't know," I shrugged.

"That is the best answer you could have," he replied. I was shocked, to say the least. "Do you believe that Jesus is the Son of God?"

"Yes," I replied.

"Do you believe that He died on the cross for your sins and was resurrected from the grave on the third day?" he asked.

"Yes, sir," I replied.

"Do you believe that Jesus is coming back for you one day?" he asked.

By this point, I was brimming with tears. "Yes, sir," I replied.

"Well, daughter, because you answered yes to all of those questions, that means that you're already saved," the pastor replied.

This conversation changed my life forever. With tears falling down my face, I hugged the pastor as my mother stood beside me proudly.

As I matured in my walk with God, I constantly battled to understand what salvation actually looks like. At times, I felt like I had an idea based on my assumptions and what my culture had taught me. There were certain behaviors that were expected of those in Christian leadership, but the congregational responsibilities and lifestyles seemed cloudy and unclear. My faith in God felt confirmed, but for years, I found myself looking for an example, a role model, or someone I could look at and *see* that God had saved them. It was difficult to find people who acted the same Sunday through Saturday. While the inconsistencies of God's people didn't turn me away from His church or Him, I was often uneasy and

11

confused about what it meant to be "saved." I was in search of someone who didn't look like the crowd. This inspired me to seek God's input. In prayer, God said to me, "I saved you – not people. If you are looking for an example, look at Me."

Growing up and maturing in my faith, I saw that I also had my share of flaws. I realized that I had ways that were not 100% righteous and holy. I knew that I had the love of Jesus in my heart, but I struggled from time to time. Knowing the struggle I fought to find a saved role model, I try to exemplify Christ in everything I do, say, or think. Again, I'm far from perfect, but I try my best to be the example someone else new to the faith can look to.

"You are the light of the world. A town built on a hill cannot be hidden. Neither do people light a lamp and put it under a bowl. Instead they put it on its stand, and it gives light to everyone in the house. In the same way, let your light shine before others, that they may see your good deeds and glorify your Father in heaven."
Matthew 5:14-16 (NIV)

This scripture reminds us that as Christians, we are not supposed to blend in with the world. Our goal is to stand out. I'm not sure if you know it or not, but when you claim to be a Christian, the spotlight turns toward you. As members of the body of Christ, the world is looking to us to see what the love of Christ looks like. They aren't just looking at what we drive, wear, or the money we can spend. They are also looking at how we love, what we say, and what we do. Jesus Christ demanded the disciples to go and make more disciples. As Christians, we have that same command. We don't just disciple through what we say or preach on a platform. **The most effective way we disciple to others is in how we live!** For this reason, it is imperative that we allow God to examine us so that we can see what we need to get rid of. This examination is not just important for us, but others as well.

PRAYER

Lord,

Help me remember what brought me to You in the first place. Help me never to forget the sacrifice You made for me. Show me my true self, full of error, yet covered by your grace. Amen.

Chapter Two
OPEN YOUR EYES

Mark 10:46-52 tells the story of a man by the name of Blind Bartimaeus. When Jesus and the disciples came into Jericho, they saw Bartimaeus sitting on the side of the road begging. When Bartimaeus heard that Jesus was close by, he began to shout for Jesus to have mercy on him. The people around him began to attempt to quiet him, and some even rebuked him. However, this did not stop Bartimaeus from crying for Jesus' attention. The disciples brought Bartimaeus to Jesus, and Jesus asked him what he needed. He told Jesus that he wanted to see. Jesus replied, "Go, your faith has healed you." The Bible says that Bartimaeus received his sight immediately and followed Jesus.

Bartimaeus was an average man, sitting on the side of the road. He didn't have a Bible or platform. In fact, the people didn't even think he deserved the attention of Jesus. Despite his predicament, he still shouted out for Jesus' attention. He had heard about Jesus, he believed what he heard, and now it was time for him to SEE Jesus. He was granted a timeless miracle, and decided to get up and follow Jesus.

Now, let's just say you know someone who is in the struggle of their life. You consider them a friend, so you do what you can for them. You may even go above and beyond to help them get out of their rut. After you've helped and encouraged them out of their struggle season, they go right back to what they were just delivered from. How would this make you feel? It would probably bring about several questions and stir up major frustration within you. You may believe that your friend is ungrateful and wasted your time. Why can't everyone be as grateful as Bartimaeus, right? This man understood that there was no point in Jesus giving him the ability to see if he was just going to remain a beggar. If only those that we care about could be as appreciative as Blind Bartimaeus.

Now, I want you to use your imagination again. This time, instead of being a friend, I want you to imagine being a parent. For those of you with children, this won't be that difficult. Imagine having a child. You see your child is headed down a dangerous road. Despite your many warnings, they still choose to keep walking down the same road. One day, they come to the end of their rope because life seems to be repeatedly beating them down and they cry out for your help. Though you know they deserve the consequences they are faced with, being the loving parent you are, you agree to help them. After you rescue them, a few days pass by, they leave you, and head right back to destruction again. How would you feel?

Well, your feelings aren't very different from those of our Father in Heaven. Time after time, He saves us. Time after time, we return to what we were rescued from. What good was it for Bartimaeus to receive his sight if he was going to continue to sit by the road? What good is it for you to ask God to do something for you if you are going to continue to sit on the pew and beg? After God does what you asked, get off the pew and follow Him relentlessly.

I have grown to love my eyes and my smile. In retrospect, both brought me grief at one point in my life. As I got older, I had often noticed that if I tilted my head to one side, my left eye would gravitate in the opposite direction of my head movement. However, if I had a focused point to look at, my eye would lock in place. After going to the doctor, I learned that I had a weak eye muscle in my left eye that should have been picked up on when I was a child. Essentially, my brain learned how to function with this error. I was under the impression that this was normal for everyone.

In October of 2015, I had surgery to realign the muscles behind both of my eyes. It was my first surgery, and I was extremely nervous. Generally speaking, I have rather poor vision without some form of corrective lens. I struggled with my vision for most of my life. Having my vision impaired even more from the surgery was discouraging. I had no way of knowing if the surgery would work. I had to trust that the doctors were competent and experienced in this area. For those few days, I sat in my dark bedroom, unable to go to school and too uncomfortable to go into public places. I felt useless and helpless. Since my vision was blurred, other people had to help me do basic tasks. My surgery gave me an even deeper revelation of Bartimaeus' story.

When we discuss his story in Bible Study or Sunday School, we talk about how the beggar received his sight, but we rarely take note of the process it took for him to receive his miracle. Being blind, he likely depended on others for everything. He waited upon others to provide his every need. He first had to be attentive to those around him. He knew that Jesus was passing by because he heard the conversations of others. Then, those same people who no doubt had to help him before, told him to be quiet when he attempted to get the help he needed to no longer be a beggar. *Isn't that crazy?* You would think those people would be quick to assist him. However, this wasn't the case.

Once Bartimaeus had Jesus' attention, he tossed his cloak to the side as he got up from the curb to approach Jesus. The cloak was symbolic of his life as a beggar. For beggars in those times, their cloaks were their shelter. Additionally, beggars would cast out their cloaks to receive alms or offerings from passersby. Bartimaeus knew he would no longer need his beggar's cloak well before he received his miracle. In the same way, we must get rid of anything that causes us to struggle in our Christian walk or is a constant reminder of what we lack. We must be willing to cast aside the baggage, dead weight, bad habits, selfishness, pride, etc. Like Bartimaeus, we must come to Jesus expecting our miracle and ready to bring God's name glory once we have received it.

As we close this chapter, I have a very important message to share: Ladies and gentlemen, it's time to turn off our internal blindness. I know you may be thinking, *"Kendra, what do you mean by internal blindness?"* Many of our struggles, should not be struggles because we already know they're wrong and unpleasing to God. There are areas in your life and/or some activities that you actively agree to participate in. You know you shouldn't be gossiping, however, you participate in the group conversation anyway. You know you should delete your social media apps and spend some time fasting and praying, but you still scroll for hours every night. Or, maybe you spend so much time taking care of other people's homes that your house is not in order. **Whatever the struggle, it's** time to stop turning a blind eye to the conviction you feel in your heart.

Are you ready to lay aside your struggles? Or, will you continue to miss the holiness exit?

PRAYER

Lord,

Thank You for opening my eyes and not leaving me in darkness. I am grateful that the miracles that were performed in Biblical times are available for me today. Amen.

Chapter Three
WHAT DO YOU THIRST FOR?

We are human, and our physical bodies have needs that must be met to sustain and remain alive. The same is true for our spiritual body.

"Blessed are those who hunger and thirst for righteousness, for they shall be satisfied."
Matthew 5:6 (NASB)

As natural beings, we tend to pursue what we think will make us happy. Sometimes, this stems from a *keeping up with the Jones'* mentality. We focus our time and financial resources on appealing to those around us. In school, we are taught that the more education we have, the more money we can make. This concept teaches us to chase money instead of pursuing purpose. I've heard teachers and relatives inquire about a child's career interest, and when the child mentions a career that does not have a high starting salary, they discourage the child's interest.

You may have experienced this very same issue growing up.

This is just one example of how we are unconsciously molded to having a desire or thirst for financial gain to satisfy our needs. Let's make this more personal. Are you constantly chasing money to get to a higher tax bracket? I know several people who aspire to make as much money as they can, and on the surface, this seems fine. Ambition is a great quality to possess. However, if you look deeper, that chase for a higher check could be draining your spiritual needs. When we crave carnal benefits over spiritual benefits, our actions reflect that.

"So let it grow, for when your endurance is fully developed, you will be perfect and complete, needing nothing."

James 1:4 (NLT)

So, what are you longing for? Perhaps, you are not seeking financial gain. Maybe you struggle to keep positive friends around you, or you feel you are constantly being used in all your relationships. Maybe you are craving the attention of another person because you thirst to be accepted and loved. Whatever is stifling your spiritual growth because you are craving it constantly, I challenge you to surrender it to God. There is no limit to what God can do. If He can look at you with all your scars and imperfections and still call you healed, He is more than able to help you in all areas of your life. Examine your desires and test them by what the Bible declares for believers. All of our decisions should reflect the thirst we have for Him.

"I thirst for God, the living God."

Psalm 42:2a (NLT)

John 4 tells the popular story of Jesus and the Samaritan woman. In the story, Jesus is returning to Galilee from Judea, and He speaks to a woman who was a citizen of Samaria. This Biblical story stands out to me for several reasons. Samaria is an area that was typically avoided by Jews, yet on Jesus' voyage, he decided to go against the normal pattern of Jewish customs and travel through Samaria. As the disciples were in the town getting food, Jesus was sitting near a well when the Samaritan woman approached to draw water. Jesus asks the woman to get him a drink of water. By sparking this conversation, Jesus crossed gender and racial barriers. This woman, being aware of the cultural boundaries that were supposed to keep Jesus from interacting with her, questioned Jesus' motive for speaking to her.

"Jesus answered her, "If you knew the gift of God and who it is that asks you for a drink, you would have asked him, and he would have given you living water."

John 4:10 (NIV)

As they converse, Jesus reveals that He is aware of the woman's past relationship and current adultery. That could seem harsh if you're not familiar with the story, but God can meet us in the middle of sinful habits and routines. **God is intentional about meeting us right where we are.** The reputation of the Samaritan woman stood out, and the likelihood of any man speaking to her, especially a Jew, was extremely slim. Now, not only was a Jew speaking to her, but the Messiah himself offered her a drink that would eternally quench her thirst.

The Samaritan woman had no clue who she was talking to. She knew that a Messiah was prophesied to come, but did not recognize that He was in her presence. Has Jesus been standing in front of you offering you what you need but your focus on material gain and your physical needs caused you to miss Him? Has your spiritual blindness caused you to be thirsty? Instead of seeking Jesus for fulfillment, have you been going back to what you know? Friend, that place will only satisfy you temporarily. You will soon be longing to have your thirst quenched again.

Do you struggle with constantly judging and looking at the flaws of others? **Understand that there is a difference in discernment and judgment.** An example of this occurred right at Jacob's well in Samaria. When the disciples returned from town with food, they were surprised to see Jesus in conversation with the

Samaritan woman. Perhaps it was her gender or her race that caused them to become unsettled. Discernment would have allowed the disciples to see the woman's need, however, because they were judgmental, they only saw the gender and cultural lines that were crossed by their interaction. This story is an extraordinary illustration of how a personal encounter with Jesus can impact a multitude of people. Because Jesus was able to touch the heart of this one woman, a village in Samaria had the opportunity to hear about Jesus and believe in Him.

Have you gotten to a place where you love Jesus and love to be around other believers, but you struggle to be amongst those who do not show any evidence of salvation? Perhaps when you make your petition to God, you should consider asking Him to show you how to be compassionate to those who are different, just as He did. Could it be that God wants you to reach individuals with your testimony, but those people are not members of your small group at church? Is it possible that God desires you to testify to that aggravating coworker, mean-spirited boss, or overly opinionated family member? Meet them at their well and share the Good News of Jesus Christ. This does not require you to call out their sins or try to shun them into accepting Jesus.

Show the love of Jesus in your actions and daily behaviors. That's where real impact takes place. It would not have been enough if Jesus had only talked about what God could offer. He expressed the will and power of the Father through His public and private life. Reaching another sector of people will cause you to be uncomfortable and stretched, but God will reap the reward. There are people waiting for you to show them the source of living water – not just another temporary resource.

Growing up, my mother always taught me to be prepared in all situations. As a result, often when I go places, I carry a bottle of water, pack of gum, and small snack. I never want to be in a place where there is not an opportunity for me to replenish myself. I feel more relaxed if I know that there is water near me. I would rather have water and not need it than not to have water and desire it. There were times that my mother would encourage me to grab water before we left the house, and I would decline only to find out later on that I needed my own beverage. After having repeated experiences with dehydration and fatigue, I decided to take the proper precautions. This habit, formed upon obedience, became a lifestyle. Although my mother was telling me to be prepared, I thought I had it figured out. I had not achieved that level of wisdom. During my periods of dehydration, I realized how much water meant to me. When my body gave me hints that I was thirsty, even if I ignored the feeling, it did not negate my body's physical need to be replenished.

When someone initially removes a fish from the water, it squirms as if its body is in a state of shock. It wiggles around because it is not familiar with an environment in which it must fight to breathe. Our environment does not allow most fish to continue to live. After being out of the water for a while, the fish suffocates because that's not the environment they were created to thrive in. I don't have to go under water to know that I cannot survive there. My physical body does not have gills that would allow me to function there. Have you taken your physical body into a place that drains your spirit? Answering this question should make you wonder if that is why you are struggling in a particular area.

At first, your spirit was trying to make you uncomfortable so that you could get to a place where your spirit could thrive. Then, for whatever reason, you got stuck, and now your spirit is suffering tremendously because of it. In this chapter, we've seen how in the midst of a physical need, God provided uniquely. The Samaritan woman went to the well to get a physical need met, but her spiritual needs were met as well.

Are you struggling because your spirit is in an environment so dry that it can't even gasp for air? Does life have you so busy that you can't give your spirit some water? Spiritual dehydration is a real state that occurs in the lives of believers. Just like a fish out of water, we should crave to be covered in the Word and Will of Jesus. Water is essential for all form of life, and our sprit is no exception. Why settle for being a dry Christian when Christ offers living water?

PRAYER

Dear Lord,

   Help me to change my desires to be what you would want for me. Provide me with grace to take care of my spiritual drought. I want my soul to be watered by your presence. Amen.

Chapter Four
WHY ME?

Have you ever been in a tight situation and asked God, *"Why me?"* This is not the part of the book where I tell you that you shouldn't ask this question. This is where I ask you to consider reframing it.

Growing up, I was considered a pleasant child. I was polite and made good grades. I do not think anyone could tell that I was unhappy, emotionally abused, and teased. I had very low self-esteem. My goal was to make it through each day. I wasn't living – only existing. Can you imagine a 9-year-old girl living like this? I knew I was a good person, but I could not understand why I was without any real friends.

"For I envied the proud when I saw them prosper despite their wickedness. They seem to live such painless lives; their bodies are so healthy and strong. They don't have troubles like other people; they're not plagued with problems like everyone else."
Psalm 73:3-5 (NLT)

For years, I struggled to understand why people who did wrong were constantly blessed. I was in a similar state as the writer of Psalm 73. To me, it felt like everyone was prospering and being blessed, but I was stuck. I would often think to myself, *"Here I am being 'a good Christian girl', but my world is rocky and all over the place,"* It got to a point when I doubted if being good was even worth the hassle. This same thought plagued me for nine years until I heard my youth pastor say this scripture:

> *"And let us not be weary in well doing: for in due season we shall reap, if we faint not."*
> Galatians 6:9 (KJV)

This scripture shook my entire world. It gave me a direct answer to what I had been looking for. It was, for me, a hidden gem in the Word. God encouraged me right then and there. Anytime I struggled with insecurities surrounding the blessings of others, I used that scripture to pray to combat the thoughts I had of myself that God did not give me. God's Word has the answer to many of the questions believers ponder over time and time again.

The answer to my *"Why me?"* really was not about me. God had to show me that I was typically alone because He was separating me. God knew that if people constantly surrounded me, I would get consumed and be too distracted to seek Him. God was showing me, even in my elementary school years, that disappointment may occur, but He can provide comfort and peace.

You may not want to hear this, but, at times, it has to hurt for God to get your attention. God may have attempted to get your attention in other ways, but perhaps they went unheard or unnoticed. He tried to get you to pray at home, but you would rather watch television and make the argument that you do not know how to pray when there are several outlines in the Bible. You attempt to be better in your relationship with God, but you still utter foul words out of the same mouth you pray with. Your finances could be rocky because you don't budget and aren't a great steward (manager) over what He has given you or, maybe God wants you to learn to depend on Him. God had to show me that my provision does not come from my job, my paystub, or any other source of income. It comes from Him and Him alone. I could work myself to the core at work and still not recognize that I needed to exert the same effort into building my relationship with Christ.

Maybe the answer to your *"Why Me?"* is that God is tired of being the only one in your relationship doing any work. It was necessary for Him to shake things up a bit so that you could pay attention to His desires for you. God cannot get to you with all that clutter in your mind and environment.

"The thief comes only to steal and kill and destroy; I have come that they may have life, and have it to the full."

John 10:10 (NIV)

Sometimes, our trouble is allowed by God just to show us our value. Thieves (the enemy) would not be bothered with you if you did not have anything valuable inside. So the answer to your, *"Why me?"* could be because God has planted so much purpose and power into you and Satan does not want you to prosper because of the glory God would get. So, he has assigned imps to you daily to distract you from pressing on towards your purpose and fulfilling your God-given goals. The enemy is very aware of the gifts God has given you, and wants you to be and feel isolated. Despite his attempts to make you feel alone, remember that God will NEVER leave or forsake you. (Deuteronomy 31:6)

As human beings, we can exert so much energy in trying to figure out why things are happening that we miss the blessing of the experience. If you are not familiar with the life of Job, I encourage you to read it. In summary, Job was considered to be an upright man, and Satan challenged God regarding Job's character. Satan thought that the only reason Job was "blameless" was because of all the good and prosperous things occurring in his life. God gave Satan permission to torment Job as long as he did not put him to death, just to prove that Job would not curse Him. Job lost his family, his finances, and his health. To top it all off, his friends and wife refused to encourage him. Job became frustrated and confused and wanted to understand why he was experiencing great pain.

Your struggle is not just for you. Job had no idea that the reason he was being tested was for God's glory. Perhaps it's for others around to be a witness to how someone of faith handles the ups and downs of life. **We must change our minds from selfish thinking to kingdom thinking.** Job's life encourages us in our error as well as our good deeds. Job had everything stripped from him, not because he was in error, but because he was a great man of faith. Job experienced great agony so that we could learn the importance of remaining faithful. The story of Job teaches us to trust God no matter what our situations may seem to be.

FIBROMYALGIA

My sophomore year in undergrad, I began experiencing sporadic pain spurts that were unexplainable. One day, I was in my stress reduction course learning about different breathing techniques. As my class was focused on the assignment, my focus was shifted to merely enduring the remaining few minutes of the class. After we were done, our professor asked if anyone in the class noticed a difference in their heart rate. Most stated that they noticed their heart rate had slowed as they were able to breathe and calm down. Meanwhile, my heart rate was increasing because I felt a burning pain forming in my lower back.

When we were dismissed, I slowly grabbed my backpack and crept towards the exit. As I approached the wooden double doors, the pain became unbearable, and I had to rely on the white brick wall to hold me up. I stood in agony and fear and fought back the tears. I didn't want to ask for help, and I didn't want anyone to see me cry. I was the strong friend, the encourager, the believer. I couldn't ask anyone for help. All I could do was lean against the wall. My professor and classmate, who had stayed back to meet with her, saw me as they headed towards the double doors. My tears ducts gave out and released a wave of tears. Until that moment, I had never understood what it felt like to have the desire to walk, but physically could not. Naturally, my teacher and classmate were concerned. They gently took my backpack off and guided me into a chair where I sat and wept. They asked me if I wanted them to contact anyone on my behalf and I declined.

At that time, I did not have medical insurance, so I was thinking from a financial place. I had aged out of the state insurance, my father was disabled, and my mother was unemployed. There were no medical benefits in place for me at the time. I really wanted to talk to my mother, but I knew she was in class; I did not want to disturb her lesson. Eventually, I told my teacher that I would be okay to walk to our school's student center. As I made my way down the ramps of the coliseum, where my class was held, I was able to get in contact with my mother. I explained to her what had happened and that I did not know what to do. I'm sure my mother could hear the panic in my voice. Little did I know, this would be the beginning of a long road for my health journey.

Each doctor's appointment I had made a negative impression on my self-esteem. I was in a low place, to the point where I refused to seek medical attention for anything. I had medical professionals accuse me of making up my symptoms because my lab results were inconsistent. I became completely disgusted by the lack of concern and follow-up for what I was experiencing. I have had people make fun of me to my face. People have even joked as if what I was experiencing was *not all that bad*. After years of medical procedures and tests, I received a diagnosis of Fibromyalgia. Fibromyalgia is a chronic pain condition that impacts muscles and joints. It causes increased fatigue and memory loss. This became another wound in my already fractured self-esteem.

As time grew on, my faith grew stronger. I thank God for my health challenges now because they taught me a lot about Him, myself, and others. On days I wish I didn't have to deal with my health circumstances, I am reminded of how much my level of compassion has grown. It also gives me another reason to praise God without restraints.

We will never 100% understand how or why God does what He does. We will also never understand who He is without studying His Word. I had to learn that my struggles were a part of God's will. While I was flustered and fighting feelings of hopelessness, God was increasing my faith, my prayer time, and my prayer substance. I have faith that God can give me complete healing, and I also believe that God can use me to bring people to His kingdom through my ailments. I have access to an entirely different population of people that I would not have had without my medical condition. The truth is, you are the perfect person to experience what you're experiencing. The next time you prepare to ask God, "Why me?" Look at yourself in the mirror and ask, "Why not me?"

PRAYER

Lord,
   We thank You for choosing us. We appreciate You for keeping Your hand on us even when we do not understand every area of our lives. Help us to remain confident in You and trust Your plan for our lives. Amen.

Chapter Five
STAY ON TASK

I n Luke 4, the Holy Spirit led Jesus into the wilderness. For starters, this lets us know that **not all spiritual moves will happen in comfortable places.** While Jesus was in the wilderness for 40 days fasting, the devil began to tempt Him. Some of us are unable to handle being tempted by a slice of cake, let alone going days without water and food, and not to mention being tempted by Satan himself. Satan asked Jesus to perform miracles and gain worldly treasure. He even manipulated the scriptures to get Jesus to fall down and worship him. But JESUS properly divided the Word of God.

"Study to shew thyself approved unto God, a workman that needeth not to be ashamed, rightly dividing the word of truth."
2 Timothy 2:15 (KJV)

Even though the enemy attempted to knock Jesus off His game and attack Him while He was weak, Jesus was prepared. Since He knew the Word of God, He was able to beat Satan at his own game. Though weak from fasting and being in the desert, Jesus refused to give in. The enemy attempted to catch Jesus slipping, just as he did Adam and Eve in the Garden of Eden. Satan clearly underestimated Jesus. As you continue to read this chapter, I would like you to ponder this thought, "What do you do when you are off the clock?"

Before we go to work, we usually complete a few tasks to prepare to operate at our best on the job. We handle our hygiene, put on the appropriate clothes, and eat a meal for energy. Now I want you to think about your preparation in a spiritual aspect. We worship God in our way, read a variety of daily devotionals, and declare affirmations to help set the tone of our day. On Sunday mornings, we prepare to experience God's presence in a corporate setting. We sing songs and play worship music to raise our expectations to see God. Once we have arrived at the job, we are TTG (Trained to Go)! We're immersed in our task or job roles. We answer phone calls, respond to our supervisors, check emails, and go in and out of meetings. Some have even learned how to separate the outside world from the work environment. We do this because we are aware that we have a job to do!

As believers, our spiritual workload includes spiritual warfare. Fasting is a spiritual discipline that is a vital part of our relationship with Christ. Fasting is a spiritual discipline that occurs when a believer makes a conscious effort to make sacrifices unto God. Fasting styles vary, yet the principles of fasting remains constant. Fasting allows us to declutter our minds and allows God to nourish our spirits. When you are working for God, discipline is needed to keep your flesh in check and edify your spirit. Additionally, while at work for the Lord, our church and prayer life are parallel. With these working elements, we get to experience intimacy with God.

The part of our spiritual work contract that can get a little tricky is that we must not get caught up in having an audience when we are doing Kingdom work. This is not to say that no one should ever see us do the work of the Lord. However, being seen must not be our only objective. Do you only give to the homeless when your peers are around? Do you only volunteer during large events at your church? Do you only want to sing with the choir when it is your turn to lead a song? Or, do you only participate in ministries that you hold a leadership position in? Do not miss the mark hoping to gain the applause of people.

There is an incomparable number of endorphins that are released when I walk out of work. I'm sure you've experienced this as well. A large portion of working people desire to relax when possible. We want to let our guards down, get comfortable, and take off our work clothes. So, when it comes to your faith, do you take off your armor as soon you leave church? We can be so full, powerful, and anointed when we are in the comforts of our church facilities, but what happens when we leave? This is not to say that we don't need to rest. Rest is needed and necessary. In fact, God's Word says that He gives rest to those He loves. (Psalm 127:2)

In the desert, Jesus was hungry and weak, but He knew He still had a job to do. He couldn't afford to give Satan any wiggle room. Just because we are not always "at work" doesn't mean we need to act like we don't have a job. In Luke 4, Jesus wasn't tempted when He was at the temple, or at His baptism. Satan waited (seeking whom he may devour) until Jesus was tired, weak, and in a vulnerable state. When you are off the clock, it is easy to become manipulated if you are not on guard.

"When the devil had finished tempting Jesus, he left him until the next opportunity came."
Luke 4:13 (NLT)

Therefore, we can never let our guards down. The enemy is sure to return the moment we are weak, not reading our Bibles, and ignoring the need to pray. We should not be surprised when we see his schemes. It's the enemy's job to wreak havoc, and he is always at work. What's your job? How's your performance? As believers, we are employed by Christ. We have different roles, but our hours are still the same. We may take an extended lunch break, but we are always on the clock. In Luke 4:1-13, Jesus provided us with the perfect example of how to combat the enemy. He showed us how to stand firm in what we KNOW about God. He teaches us to resist the urge to give in to what seems like a temporary solution to our problem. Finally, His actions remind us to rely on the scriptures that are hidden in our hearts. So, what should we do when we are off the clock of our spiritual job? Clock back in, get back to work, and stay on task!

PRAYER

Lord,

Help your children to be prepared for work. Help us to never stop working to build Your Kingdom. You have given us all tasks that need to be fulfilled. God, we thank You for giving us assignments and we ask for your help to complete them. Amen.

Chapter Six
SHOOT YOUR SHOT

When I was younger, my mother thought it was important that I learn how to swim, so one summer, she signed me up for swim camp. Swim camp was full of surprises and new adventures for me. During this camp, we learned the fundamentals of breathing, how our body floats, how to remain calm in the water, breaststrokes, and other swimming techniques and strategies. The teacher was gentle and patient with each of us. As a group, we each had to pass a variety of tasks to be able to move to the next level. One morning after our normal swim lessons, our teacher gave each of us inflatable armbands and challenged us to jump into the 8 feet side of the pool and swim to the other side. Upon hearing her instructions, I was instantly filled with fear and nervousness. When I looked around and realized my entire class would be watching, I went into stage 4

KENDRA SIMS

anxiety. A lump formed in my throat and the rate of my heart beat increased.

As I sat and watched each of my peers jump in, I grew even more nervous. I let everyone go ahead of me to mask my fear and give myself more time to jump in. When my turn finally came, I could not do it. I tried to psych myself out, but nothing seemed to work. I wanted to find the courage to conquer my fear, but I couldn't find one drop. My mother offered encouragement that eventually turned into frustration. She was visibly disappointed in me, and I had feelings of guilt and negative emotions. My mother even gave me a pep talk in the car to convince me to give it another try. All I could do was cry tears of frustration.

That following week, the last week of swim camp, our teacher presented us with the same scenario, but this time, we had to do it without the inflatable armbands. Though I still felt defeated from the last week, I realized I had another chance to face my fear. When my turn came, I tip-toed to the edge of the pool, bent my trembling knees, and jumped into the pool. As I became engulfed in the rushing waters, I began to feel like a conqueror. A satisfying sense of relief and accomplishment overwhelmed me as I swam across the pool. I was so proud of myself. In just one week, I gained the courage to ignore my fear and shoot my shot! I enjoyed every second of it and wished I had done it sooner.

44

As I think back on those weeks in summer camp, I can't figure out why I was so terrified to jump. I was protected, and I knew my teacher was right there to jump in if I needed her. I was so afraid of the pool that I forgot to trust my teacher. I saw her the entire time. I knew she had given me the tools and prepared me to take on the task. The fear of *"what if"* stopped me from reaching my goal sooner.

What about you? What have you been afraid of? Could your current struggle be over if you were to stop being afraid to take a leap of faith? Jesus didn't allow himself to be beaten, humiliated, and hung on the cross just so that we can live lives full of regret and wishful thinking. **Your miracle is on the other side of the obstacle that scares you.** Cross over the fear boundary and get the blessings that await you!

How often does God present us with life-altering opportunities? He presents them daily. Stop making excuses, shoot your shot, and jump into the pool! Jumping in requires faith. It requires you to let go and trust God to keep you.

As we completed our challenge, my swim teacher did not stand on the sideline. She was in the water with us. Though she did not hold us, she swam right beside us. Even though I had been taught, I still found peace in knowing that my teacher was right beside me. If my own ability failed me, I knew the one who instructed me was not far away. In the same way, our Heavenly

Father is right there with us during every leap of faith. How gracious is that? God meets us exactly where we are. Regardless of your level of faith and spirituality, He is still there to lead and give you instruction. God loves us enough to stay in the water with us, comfort us, and pull us up if we begin to sink. Isn't that so comforting?! Now that you know Jesus is in the pool, you have no reason to hold back! Jump, my friend. Jump!

> *"The LORD himself goes before you and will be with you; he will never leave you nor forsake you. Do not be afraid; do not be discouraged."*
> Deuteronomy 31:8 (NIV)

> *"So do not fear, for I am with you; do not be dismayed, for I am your God. I will strengthen you and help you; I will uphold you with my righteous right hand."*
> Isaiah 41: 10 (NIV)

PRAYER

Lord,
  Help me to replace fear with faith in You. Help me to get out of my own way and trust You in every area of my life. Lord, I want to let my guard down and shoot my shot of faith with You. I want to trust You. Help me to hold on to You as You guide me through life. Help me to continue to accept Your will! Amen.

Chapter Seven
COME BACK TO GOD

Zechariah was a prophet. There is an entire book in the Bible about him. Its message is rooted in the people's need to return to the Lord. The Book of Zechariah serves as a reminder that there is great hope in the Lord for people who follow Him. But, what happens when that hope requires you to do something that you don't like or particularly care for? As believers, there are three changes that we need to work on actively: accepting the truth, actively pursue God, and adjusting our lifestyle.

"God was very angry with your ancestors. So give to the people this Message from God-of-the-Angel-Armies: 'Come back to me, and I'll come back to you. Don't be like your parents. The old-time prophets called out to them, "A Message from God-of-the-Angel-Armies: Leave your evil life. Quit your evil practices." But they ignored everything I said to them, stubbornly refused to listen. And where are your ancestors now? Dead and buried. And the prophets who preached to them? Also

dead and buried. But the Message that my servants the prophets spoke, that isn't dead and buried. That Message did its work on your ancestors, did it not? It woke them up and they came back, saying, 'He did what he said he would do, sure enough. We didn't get by with a thing.'"

Zechariah 1: 2-6 The Message

In the scripture, the people who had returned from Babylonian exile had been issued a warning to return to God. (See Verses 3-4) So, we know that they had been given the truth. They knew what NOT to do.

These scriptures are a message to believers today to learn from the mistakes of those who came before us. We do not have to be like those individuals who lie, are lazy, or consistently make the wrong decisions. These characteristics may be in some of our friends, people we know, or even ourselves. It is not too late. You can go back to school, and you can give your body back to God! Like the people of God in Zechariah 1:2-6, you too are without an excuse!

When I was growing up, I was considered a good student. I did what I was told, completed assignments, and was not disruptive in class. This does not mean that I always felt like being a good student, but I knew that if I wanted to survive in my mother's house, there were rules I had to follow. This was my truth! My mother's rules could be summed up into two categories: *I had to act like I had some sense* (use my best behavior and best judgment at all times) and *make excellent grades!* If either of those two got out of order, there would be some consequences. Why? I knew what my mother expected and what would happen if she found out I had done something out of character.

Occasionally, if I got caught talking in class, as I often did because I would swiftly finish my work, my teacher would grant a warning. One day, my teacher caught me talking in class, and when he called on me, I told him that I was not the only person talking. At this moment, it was not a matter of who was right and who was wrong, but a matter of respect. I didn't intend to be disobedient. Although I was not alone in this deed, I was still caught doing something that was frowned upon. This one action was a direct violation of rule number one in my household, *"Act like you have some sense."* I knew my mom would not be pleased when she found out, but I also felt like it wasn't fair for me to get in trouble if I was not the only one doing wrong.

Isn't that how we rationalize our behaviors? If we aren't the only people doing it, it's okay or not that bad. As a child of God, we live in His house, which means that we need to abide by His rules regardless of what others are doing. Do you actually know the rules of God? Do you really know Him or are you just using His Words? Do your decisions match the Word of God? James 2:17 says that faith without works is dead. Faith and action work together! So, ask yourself: Does your music playlist match the Word of God? Do your text messages match the Word of God? Do your recent financial transactions match the Word of God? *DOES YOUR INTERNET SEARCH HISTORY MATCH THE WORD OF GOD?*

> *"The Lord rewarded me according to my righteousness."*
>
> Psalm 18: 20 (HCSB)

In this era, we seem to have a pattern of wanting the benefits of God, without putting in the work. We want the benefits of being a leader, but don't want to go through leadership training. We want the following of big-name celebrities, but we don't want to walk in their shoes. We want a spouse, but are we willing to put in the WORK being happily single with Jesus and functioning as His bride?

In the passage at the beginning of the chapter, the people in Babylonian exile were given clear instructions from God: *Leave your evil life and quit your evil practices.* These two instructions can seem simple if we only stay on the surface. I have a few questions that I would like you to think about:

- What happens when evil practices seem to be a normal occurrence in our everyday lives?
- What happens when our evil practices involve the people who we communicate with regularly? Ex. Our shopping habits, those

lottery tickets, or even browsing the internet for hours yet neglecting to read the Bible. Let's go back to the story of when my teacher singled me out for talking. As you probably guessed, my teacher told my mom what occurred. When I saw my mom at the end of the school day, she *got me together* in her unique way. Then, she made me walk with her to apologize to my teacher. I honestly was not sorry at all. I just knew I had to *"act like I had some sense."* This moment served as a reminder that my mother required me to follow her rules if I desired to remain in her home.

Sometimes, God has to remind us that He is going to do what He said He would do. When He does this, it causes us to remember how real and present God is. When we have this realization within ourselves, we begin to ponder how and why we should *get it together.* This mostly happens when a loved one dies, we receive bad grades at the end of a school term, someone we care about is extremely sick, or other things of that nature. When this occurs, we tend to feel like we want and need God to *show Himself.* In moments like these, we ask ourselves questions like, *"Why does this has to happen to me?"* Or, *"Why do I have to keep going through this over and over again?"* Usually, we experience repetitive situations because we haven't learned our lesson. **God allows calamity to hit our lives to mature us, not to harm us.** NEWS

FLASH: You can switch majors, jobs, churches, cars, men, or women as many times as you desire. However, until you activate your faith and ask God for direction, you have not yet learned and are sure to repeat the lesson until you do.

When I was caught talking in class, I was only thinking about what was happening at that moment. On the other hand, my mother viewed the entire picture. It was imperative for me to learn to have and show respect for adults and authority. Though the situation was small, it taught me a big lesson: *Know when commentary is needed and when speaking will only stir confusion.* Don't forsake the lessons you learn, even in disobedience.

THE WORD VS. THE WORLD

There are many misconceptions that the world teaches us that are not in alignment with God's Word. As we go after God, we must adjust ourselves according to what God's rules are. If we do not watch what's occurring, we can get caught up in what the world has going on. So, it is imperative that we be mindful of our physical and spiritual surroundings. Before we close this book, let's bust a few myths with the Word of God.

The world encourages us to have an *"only God can judge me"* mentality. We use this as an excuse to live any way we feel. While no man can judge another, here's what the Word says about our accountability to one another as believers.

"Therefore confess your sins to each other and pray for each other so that you may be healed. The prayer of a righteous person is powerful and effective."

James 5:26 (NIV)

The world says that it's okay to not go to church because of all the hypocrites that attend. Without being mindful, we can forget that Jesus came for the sick and the church is where people come to get healed.

"On hearing this, Jesus said to them, "It is not the healthy who need a doctor, but the sick. I have not come to call the righteous, but sinners."

Mark 2:17 (NIV)

The world may say you don't have to give your money to the church. That is not what the Word says. When you neglect to pay your tithes, you will in some manner have to spend that money anyway. (Car trouble, higher insurance rates, home appliance, unexpected expense, etc.) I don't know about you, but I would rather it be my choice to give it God than to be forced to give it out of my disobedience.

"Bring the whole tithe into the storehouse, that there may be food in my house. Test me in this," says the Lord Almighty, "and see if I will not throw open the

floodgates of heaven and pour out so much blessing that there will not be room enough to store it."
Malachi 3:10 (NIV)

The world says that it's okay to go out, drink, smoke, and cuss as long as it does not hurt anyone, but that's not what the Word says.

"For the grace of God has appeared that offers salvation to all people. It teaches us to say "No" to ungodliness and worldly passions, and to live self-controlled, upright and godly lives in this present age."
Titus 2:11-12 (NIV)

The world says that gossip is okay as long as they don't find out who told, but that is not what the Word says.

"Do not conform to the patterns of this world but be transformed by the renewing of your mind.
Romans 12:2 (NIV)

Just as Paul admonishes us in Romans 12:2, don't fall for the hype of the world! As a believer, get into God's Word for yourself. This is the manual by which we as believers must live.

Our minds are so powerful and connected to our spirits, but we must be intentional about what we feed it. When we're going through something, it can feel like the people who are undeserving are flourishing, but fret not, the enemy will NOT win in the end. Job

24:24 states that their "rise" is momentary. So, we have to spend less time on the accolades of others and focus on the goals God has designed for us to attain. When we age spiritually and in years, certain developmental stages are supposed to take place. When you grow up, typically you reach different levels of maturity. Young children have patterns of whining, complaining, and tattle telling. It makes no sense to be an adult, but spend our days acting like children. As we mature in Christ, when we become aware of traits that do not align up with what the Word says, there should be a shift in those characteristics. There is a cliché that says, *"When you know better you do better."* Unfortunately, this is not always true. We have patterns of running to the same old mess, same old complaints, and same old situations that caused us tribulation in the first place.

On my journey, I have noticed Christians who try to "fit" God into their schedule. They say things like, *"Let's see if I will have time to get to church."* Or, they spend countless hours at church during the week, but can't recall the last time they opened their Bible in their own home. These same set of people will prioritize their lives to attend a concert. They will clear their schedules, take off work, find a babysitter, find an outfit, buy hair, and get their makeup done for a three-hour show, yet, struggle to read a daily devotional.

Some of us do not consult God fully because we don't want to know what God has to say. We like living in our comfortable, sinful routines and are afraid of change. Being afraid of change can potentially cause us to live with regrets. In my pursuit to do what God wants, I learned to release of my personal desires. We cannot be in pursuit of God if we are wasting our days in bed, gossiping on the phone, scrolling on Instagram, or overeating at fast food restaurants. When will we recognize what God is saying to us about us? When will we stop merely regurgitating what we have heard others say?

Salvation is not a cure for struggling, but we should find comfort in knowing that our doctor is on-call. Remember, it is healthy to admit to yourself that you struggle in certain areas. However, these struggles can take root and leave you feeling stagnant if not dealt with. You must invest your time in seeking the Will of God consistently. **Wake up and realize that your delayed obedience is still disobedience.** When will we quit our evil practices and return to the Father? Again I ask, what good is it for you to be a Christian if you are going to be lukewarm? You say you love Him, now what will you do about it?

PRAYER

Lord,

Thank You for the struggles in our lives that remind us how much we need You. Help us always to seek you in the middle of every life storm. Teach us to be obedient to you by aligning our goals and aspirations with Your will. Provide hope where it is lacking. Lord, we even ask that You would get into that secret prayer request we won't ask anyone to intercede for. Help us in the places where we are too ashamed to mention that we struggle. Psalms 3:3 reminds us that You lift up our heads, therefore we can walk with eyes fixated on your promises. Amen.

AKNOWLEDGEMENTS

Veronica Whitehead, thanks for being a mom who taught me how to reach for the stars and to not allow my voice to be silenced.

Jerrica Russaw, thank you for investing in my vision, and reminding me that through Christ, I can do all things.

Eddie Walton III, thank you for continuously speaking life into my dream and being the voice of reason when I had doubts.

Melanie & Taylor, thank you for allowing me to be vulnerable and share my fears, concerns, and hopes with you guys.

ABOUT THE AUTHOR

Kendra Sims was born and raised in the Atlanta metropolitan area and fell in love with Jesus throughout her years in elementary school. She felt drawn by God as a child as her interest in faith grew. Kendra officially accepted Jesus as her Lord and Savior at age 10, and she was baptized fully aware that He was to be her comfort at all times. Kendra was raised by her mother, Veronica, and stepfather, Frank, who instilled in her the importance of speaking up for herself and following her passion. Growing up, Kendra participated in cheerleading, pageants, bands, choirs, steps teams, as well as dance teams.

Kendra has a bachelor's degree from Auburn University in Human Development and Family Studies. While there, she pledged Delta Sigma Theta Sorority, Incorporated. While pursuing her graduate degree, Kendra became a licensed minister in Riverdale, GA. She has a Master of Social Work Degree from Georgia State University, where she was able to study abroad in 4 countries in Europe. Kendra currently works in Los Angeles, California as a Social Worker for foster youth.

Kendra understands that she is far from perfection, but knows that God loves her with her imperfections. Throughout her entire life, she struggled with acceptance and wanting to fit in. While battling self-esteem and self-worth, God showed Kendra that He created her in His image. Kendra has had many loved ones pass away, including her biological father, John, but in moments of grief and sadness, she sees God's light and purpose. Kendra's mission in life is to remind others that there is a reason to be hopeful in all circumstances!

STAY CONNECTED

Thank you for purchasing, *I'm Saved, but I Struggle.* Kendra would like to connect with you! Below are a few ways you can connect with Kendra, stay updated on new releases, speaking engagements, and more.

FACEBOOK Kendra-Pooh Sims
FACEBOOK Secure in Christ
INSTAGRAM @poohsmiles
INSTAGRAM @iamsecureinchrist
WEBSITE secureinchrist.com
EMAIL kendrasims_17@yahoo.com

91438840R00039